Text by Michael Prince

A New Guide Book to

Washington D.C.

8

**INTINERARIES
ILLUSTRATED BY OVER 80
COLOR PHOTOS
A COMPLETE TOUR OF THE
CITY AND ITS SURROUNDINGS
"NEW" INCLUDES OVER 90
INTERNET ADDRESSES**

Published by L.B. Prince Company

Index of Chapters

New Guide to
WASHINGTON D.C.
8 Tours with 80 Photos/City Maps
New: Over 90 Internet Addresses Included

Building, 14) Watergate Complex, 15) George Washington University, 16) National Geographic Society Headquarters, 17) Kennedy Center

5

TOUR 5:
1) National Archives, 2) U.S. Navy Memorial, 3) Post Office Pavilion, 4) F.B.I. Headquarters, 5) Martin Luther King Library, 6) Ford's Theater/Lincoln Museum, 7) National Museum of American Art, 8) National Portrait Gallery

6

TOUR 6:
1) Art Galleries, 2) Georgetown Park, 3) Georgetown University, 4) C & O Canal, 5) Washington Harbour, 6) Dunbarton Oaks

7

TOUR 7:
1) Arlington National Cemetery, 2) Custis Lee Mansion (Arlington House), 3) Women in Military Memorial, 4) Tomb of the Unknown Soldier, 5) John F. Kennedy Grave, 6) Arlington Memorial Amphitheater, 7) Netherlands Carillon 8) U.S. Marine Corps War Memorial, 9) Pentagon, 10) Ronald Reagan Washington National Airport, 11) Newseum, 12) Air Force Memorial

8

TOUR 8:
1) Ramsay House, 2) Stabler-Leadbeater Apothecary Shop, 3) Old Presbyterian Meeting House, 4) The Athenaeum, 5) The Torpedo Factory Art Center, 6) Carlyle House, 7) Market Square/City Hall, 8) Gadsby's Tavern Museum, 9) Boyhood Home of Robert E. Lee, 10) Lee-Fendall House 11) Lloyd House, 12) Christ Church 13) The Lyceum, 14) Friendship Veterans Fire Engine Association, 15) Black History Resource Center, 16) Alexandria Waterfront Museum, 17) George Washington Masonic Memorial, 18) Fort Ward Museum and Historic Site, 19) Washington's Grist Mill, 20) Gunston Hall Plantation, 21) Woodlawn Plantation and Frank Lloyd Wright's Pope-Leighey House, 22) Mount Vernon

THE STORY OF WASHINGTON, D. C.

The efforts of Thomas Jefferson and Alexander Hamilton were extremely instrumental during the controversy for the proposed site of a capital city. Many attempts had failed owing to the political rivalry between the states. Between 1783 and 1790 Congress considered various sites for the new National Capital, once authorizing work on a site near Trenton, N.J. and later choosing Germantown, PA., while settling down in Philadelphia as the temporary capital. In 1790 when the South threatened secession over the matter, Jefferson and Hamilton reached a compromise: Jefferson would back Hamilton's proposal for Federal assumption of state war debts if Hamilton would back a Potomac site for the capital. Both bills passed and President Washington selected a site of 10 square miles lying on both sides of the Potomac River. The northern part was ceded by Maryland and the southern by Virginia. Later, the southern portion was returned to Virginia and the "Territory of Columbia" became the city of "Washington".

President George Washington chose Paris-born Pierre Charles L'Enfant to design the city. L'Enfant was an engineer in the Continental Army, and patterned the city in part on the splendid expanses of Versailles. He chose Capitol Hill as the focal point and laid out broad avenues which radiate like the spokes of a wheel from centers placed within the rectangular pattern of streets. Although L'Enfant's handsome plan was in the end changed a great deal, his wide avenues and sweeping vistas, combined with monumental buildings, make the Capital unique among American cities.

In 1800 the Nation's Capital was officially moved to Washington from Philadelphia. On August 24, 1814, the British took the city and over the next few days burned all the public buildings except the combined post and patent offices. The White House was rebuilt by 1817 and two years later the Capitol Building was ready for use again.

The city's population grew rapidly. In 1840 it was 44,000, and by 1860 the population had reached 75,000. Today, Washington has a population of over 750,000 people, about two-thirds of whom work for the Federal Government.

As L'Enfant had planned Washington has vast acreage of parks, squares, circles and open space. While it is important as the center of our Federal Government, it also has become a great cultural center. It now has numerous museums, art galleries, libraries, shrines, churches, parks and monumental buildings. It is no wonder that each year millions of visitors from all parts of the world come to see this magnificent city, almost 200 years old, but so richly endowed with American history.

TOURIST INFORMATION

WCVA
Tourist information is available from the Washington D.C.
Convention and Visitor Association. 14th and Pennsylvania Avenue
N.W. 202-789-7000 http://www.washington.org

CURRENCY EXCHANGE
Deak International, Ltd. offers currency exchange on more than
120 currencies. It has over-the-counter currency service, cashes
traveller's checks in dollars or foreign currency, and cashes foreign
checks. The three branches in Washington D.C. are Union Station
(9-5 Mon. - Sa.; 12-6 Su.), Georgetown Park (10-9 Mon. - Fri.; 10-7
Sa.; 12-6 Su.), and 1800 K Street (9-5 Mon. - Fri.). Information 202-
338-3325.

IVIS
In an emergency it is possible to speak with someone in any language and be interpreted. IVIS is located at 733 15th Street N.W.
and is open 9:00am-5:00pm Monday through Friday. Call the
International Visitors Information Service 202-783-6540.

GETTING AROUND IN WASHINGTON D.C.
Washington D.C. is divided into four sections. They are formed
by the intersection of North Capitol Street, East Capitol Street, South
Capitol Street, and the Mall to the west. In the center of this intersection is our U. S. Capitol Building. The quadrants make up the
northeast, northwest, southeast and southwest areas of Washington
D.C. All addresses have an abbreviation of the section in it; i.e., NE,
NW, SE, SW. Streets that go north and south are numbered starting
from the Capitol. Streets going east and west are lettered. This is
also starting from the Capitol; however, there are no A or B Streets
west of the Capitol and Independence Avenue takes the place of B
street to the South and Constitution Avenue substitutes for B street in
the Northeast and Northwest quadrants. Also missing is J street.
East-West streets after the alphabet are 2 and 3 syllable names of
flowers and trees in alphabetical order. Any streets that run diago-
nally are named for the states, the most well-known being
Pennsylvania Ave. N.W., the Presidential inaugural route.

AIRPORTS
Washington D.C. is serviced by three commercial airports: Ronald
Reagan Washington National Airport , Dulles International Airport,
and Baltimore-Washington International Airport. http://www.met-
washairports.com. Internet travel assistance may be obtained from

TRANSPORTATION

QuickAid, http://www.quickaid.com.

METRO

The Washington Metrorail is a model subway system. The cars are luxurious, quiet and comfortable. Metrorail opened in 1976 and currently serves 75 stations along 92 miles of track, having 5 lines. Proposed are additional stations and track to bring the totals to 83 stations and 103 miles of track. For visitors, Metrorail is safe, convenient and the best way to get around in Washington D.C. Family tour passes are available for weekdays and holidays. This pass is good for any station all day for the date stamped and can be purchased in advance. There is supplimental bus service to areas not covered by the metrorail system. Operating Hours: M-F 5:30am-12midnight; Sa. 8am-12midnight; Sundays & Holidays 10am-12midnight. Information: 202-637-7000

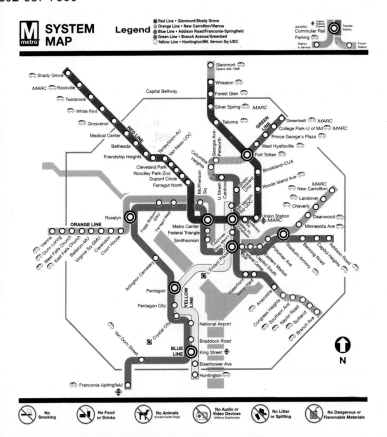

TOURS
Some, but not necessarily all tours are:
    All About Town Tours 202-393-3696
    Arlington Visitor Service 703-358-3988
    Bike The Sites Inc. 202-966-8662. http://www.bikethesites.com
    Blue Line Sightseeing 202-529-7755.
    C&O Canal Barge Rides: 301-739-4200
    Capital Entertainment Services 202-636-9203
    Double Decker Bus Tours 202-944-9700
    Federal City Tours 800-778-7373 http://www.fctours.com/fct/
    Gray Line Information 202-479-5900
    Guided Walking Tours of Washington 301-294-9514
    Liberty Helicopter Tours & Charter 301-484-8484
    Odyssey Cruises 202-488-6000 http://www.odyssey-cruises.com
    Old Town Trolley 202-269-3020
    Scandal Tours 301-587-4291
    Thrifty Tours 703-924-9400
    TOURMOBILE 202-554-7950 http://www.tourmobile.com

RENTAL CARS
Some Rental agencies, but not necessarily all are:
    AVIS 800-331-1212
    Budget 703-521-8137
    Dollar 703-661-6888
    Enterprise 703-448-8183
    Pohanka   301-899-7000
    Thrifty   703-941-9520

MUSIC CONCERTS
Some Ticket Companies for various Music Concerts are:
    http://www.ascticket.com
    http://www.ticketfinders.com
    http://www.tourdates.com

A variety of web-sites offer Washington D.C. guides:
http://www.aals.org/cityinfo.html;
http://imagesite.com/muse/museylpgs.html
http://www.nationalparks.org
http://www.washington.org
http://www.discovery.com/destnationdc
http://www.bot.org
http://atevo.com
http://chesbaynet.com

Tour I: Capitol Hill

*1.) Children's Museum, 2.) National Postal Museum,
3.) Union Station, 4.) U.S. Capitol Building,
5.) Library of Congress, 6.) Supreme Court, 7.) Folge*
Shakespeare Library, 8.) U.S. Botanic Gardens

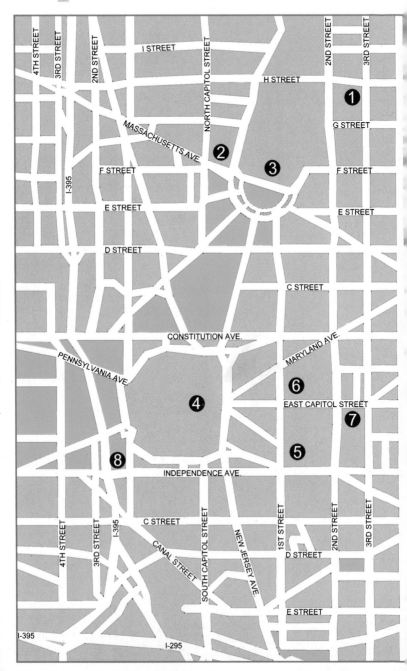

● CAPITAL CHILDREN'S MUSEUM

A visit to the Capital Children's Museum at 800 3rd Street N.E. behind Union Station is a wonderful and fun place for children from 2-12 years of age. All of the exhibits are made to be handled. A City room is designed to help children learn how to use the city with cars to drive and uniforms to dress up in. There is a permanent exhibit on Mexico that includes an open-air market where kids can put on ponchos and sombreros and stroll the marketplace. There is a sculpture garden by Nek Chand. An exhibit chronicling the development of communication from an Ice Age Cave to satellite communication. The future center allows children to learn about the world of computers. The Capital Children's Museum also sponsors professional and amateur groups for children's theater. This is a great place for kids to learn while having fun. It is open 10 to 5 daily, closed Thanksgiving, Christmas, New Year's Day, and Easter.
Information 202-543-8600.

❷ NATIONAL POSTAL MUSEUM

See Tour 2: Smithsonian Institution.

❸ UNION STATION

Perhaps the most pleasant way to arrive in Washington D.C. is by Amtrak which pulls into this monumental old station. The concourse is the largest room in the world—750 ft long and 130 feet wide. Union Station is an historical monument renowned for the number of soldiers passing through in war. The cornerstone was laid in 1905; it was opened in 1907 and completed in 1908. Browse among the three levels and over 100 shops including a food court and movie theater. The station itself is open 24 hours while the shops are open 9am-8pm Monday through Saturday, and noon-6pm Sunday. There is a five level parking garage in back with two hours free parking (see information desk for ticket validation). 30-45 minute free tours are available. When you emerge from the Station, you're greeted by a stunning view of the Plaza and Capitol Building. http://www.trainweb.com

❹ U.S. CAPITOL BUILDING

President Washington laid the cornerstone in 1793 and seven years later, Congress met there for the first time. By 1859, the House and Senate extensions were added.

During the Civil War the dome was completed. During the early months of the Civil War, the Capitol was used as a barracks for Northern troops. The House and Senate Chambers, Statuary Hall, the Rotunda, the Crypt, and the President's Room are the most interesting.

The Rotunda and Statuary Hall contain art works immortalizing American History and the Americans who were a part of it. Final tribute to 27 Americans including four Presidents has been paid in the Capitol Rotunda. The Capitol is connected with the Senate Office Buildings and the House Office Buildings by underground passageways and subway systems. The huge illuminated dome is a beautiful spectacle at

get to see a session of full Congress since most of the work done by your representatives is done in committee. The domed Capitol Building is probably the most recognized and familiar architectural outline in America. http://www.house.gov; http://www.senate.gov; & http://www.uschs.org

night. The building has no back, but rather, east and west fronts. It is 287' 5 1/2" tall, 350' wide and over 751' long with a floor area of 16 1/2 acres. Yet even this is not sufficient for the business of government since there are six additional buildings containing offices and committee rooms for the House and Senate.

These additional buildings are Cannon, Longworth, Rayburn, Russell, Kirksen, and Hart. The Capitol is open every day except Christmas, New Year's, and Thanksgiving. Guided tours are available from 9:00am-3:45pm daily. When you visit the Capitol, please be patient with the security; there have been two bomb explosions in the building (1971 and 1983). Do not be surprised if you do not

⑤ LIBRARY OF CONGRESS

The Library of Congress, originally located in the U.S. Capitol, is now comprised of three buildings just east of the Capitol. The Thomas Jefferson building, completed in 1897, shows the influence of the Italian Renaissance. The John Adams Building opened in 1939 and the James Madison Building was completed in 1980. Among the 90 million books, periodicals, films and manuscripts included in the collection are priceless examples of Americana dating to the 17th Century. Jefferson's own draft of the Declaration of Independence and Europe's treasure, the Gutenberg Bible, are on permanent display here. 2/3 of the books present are in a language other than English.

The Library serves as the research and reference arm of Congress although it is open to the public. Requests for information from Representatives are handled by the Congressional Research Service which processes approximately 450,000 inquiries a year. The Library is administered by the Librarian of Congress who is appointed by the President and confirmed by the Senate. No books may be checked out, but they are available for reading in the 22 reading rooms. In the case of some rare books, inter-library loans may be arranged. Another function of the library is the copyright office located in the James Madison Building. The Library does not keep a copy of all books published in the United States. The acids used in paper manufacture over the last century are causing many books to turn to dust. The Library is devoted to preserving these books. A fifteen minute movie about the Library is shown at quarter till the hour every hour from 8:45am-8:45pm weekdays; 8:45am-5:45pm weekends and holidays in the Jefferson Building. Guided tours are available from 10am-3pm Monday through Friday.

The Library itself is open every day except Christmas and New Year's; All public exhibits except Madison Gallery and the Great Hall are open 9:00am-5:30pm daily. The other two are open Monday-Friday: 8:30am-9:30pm; Saturday: 8:30am-6:30pm; Sunday and Holidays: 1:00pm-5:00pm. Information 202-707-6400. For events calendar call 202-707-2905.
http://www.loc.gov

⑥ SUPREME COURT

Sixteen columns of Vermont marble support the main entrance to this classic, Greek- designed building that houses the highest court in the land. The building, just east of the Capitol, was started in 1932 and completed in 1935. It is 385' by 304'. Here the laws of our country receive a final inter- pretation. In the Great Hall are busts of former Chief Justices.

Other exhibits are to be seen; some are permanent while others are travelling. Also featured is a 20 minute film about the grounds and history of the Supreme Court. When court is not in session there are court- room lectures hourly from 9:30am-3:30pm. The court is in session hearing arguments from October to June on Monday, Tuesday and Wednesday from 10:00 A.M. to Noon and 1:00 to 3:00 P.M. These sessions are open to the public, but there is seating for only 200. On the day of arguments, the Washington Post publishes a brief description of each case. The Supreme Court is open 9:00am-4:25pm Monday through Friday and closed weekends and holidays.
Information 202-479-3211.

⑦ THE FOLGER SHAKE- SPEARE LIBRARY

Located at 201 E. Capitol Street, this is probably

America's greatest tribute to Shakespeare. Through the generosity of Henry Clay Folger, much of the spirit of Elizabethan England has been recreated here, including a Shakespearean Theater suggestive of an inyard. The Library, administered by the trustees of Amherst College, houses the world's largest collection of Shakespearean literature and is only open to researchers who have obtained the appropriate credentials in advance. There are exhibits of books, manuscripts, artwork, and memorabilia such as theatrical playbills and costume jewelry open to the public. Tours are available Monday through Saturday from 11:00 am to 1:00pm. The library exhibits are open 10am-4pm. Monday through Saturday; closed Sunday and Federal holidays. The Library also sponsors over 100 public programs a year from chamber music to poetry and fiction readings.
Information 202-544-7077.
http://www.folger.edu

⑧ U.S. BOTANIC GARDEN

The Botanic Garden, at the foot of the Capitol, houses a well-maintained permanent collection of both exotic and familiar plants. From September to June, the staff of the Botanic Garden offers a series of horticultural classes on specific plants. A total of 9,000 square feet of exhibition hall features approximately 5,000 species and varieties from around the world, including a Bunya-bunya Tree from Australia.

The Botanic Garden features seasonal flower shows including a summer terrace, a chrysanthemum, and two Christmas shows. The gardens are open daily 9am-5pm; although for June, July, and August the hours are extended to 9am-9pm.
Information 202-225-7099.

TOUR 2: Smithsonian Institution

On The Mall: 1.) Arthur M. Sackler Gallery, 2.) Arts and Industries Building, 3.) Enid A. Haupt Garden, 4.) Freer Gallery of Art, 5.) Hirshhorn Museum and Sculpture Garden, 6.) National Air and Space

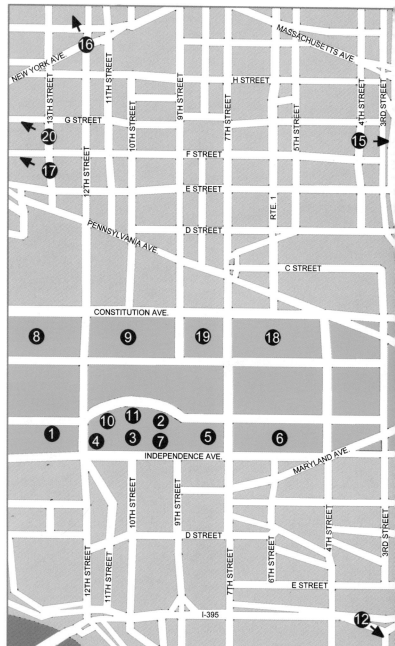

Museum, 7.) *National Museum of African Art,* 8.) *National Museum of American History,* 9.) *National Museum of Natural History,* 10.) *S. Dillon Ripley Center (International Gallery),* 11.) *Smithsonian Institution Building (The Castle).*

Off The Mall: 12.) *Anacostia Museum,* 13.) *National Museum of American Art,* 14.) *National Postal Museum,* 15.) *National Portrait Gallery,* 16.) *National Zoo,* 17.) *Renwick Gallery.*

The Smithsonian Institution is the largest museum complex in the world. Its 14 museums display only a tiny fraction of the 135 million artifacts held in trust. The Smithsonian is also dedicated to public education, national service and scholarship in the arts, sciences and history. It sponsors many concerts, lectures, and other public programs including the Festival of American Folk-life. The institution was established in 1846. Your visit to the Nation's Capital is incomplete without seeing the museums of the Smithsonian. All but one (the Cooper-Hewitt Museum in New York) are in Washington. Literature is available in English, Japanese, Chinese, German, Spanish, French, and Arabic. The Mall Museums are open from 10am - 5:30pm daily except December 25, with extended summer hours determined annually. Information (recorded): 202-357-2020; (in person) 202-357-2700. http://www.si.edu

Administered Separately: 18.) National Gallery of Art, 19.) National Gallery of Art, Sculpture Garden, 20.) John F. Kennedy Center of Performing Arts

❶ ARTHUR M. SACKLER GALLERY

This gallery at 1050 Independence Ave. S.W. specializes in Asian Art. Dr. Arthur Sackler, a New York medical researcher, publisher and art collector, donated over 4 million dollars to the construction of the building as well as hundreds of pieces of Asian art. His intention was not only to exhibit Asian masterpieces but to establish a center for research, fellowship awards and publications. In addition to the permanent exhibits there are visiting exhibitions. Be sure to see Chinese jades and bronzes, near Eastern gold as well as Persian manuscripts.

❷ ARTS AND INDUSTRIES BUILDING

When the Centennial Exhibition closed in Philadelphia in 1876, most of the states and foreign exhibitors found it cheaper to donate their exhibits to the United States government than to ship them home. Congress then voted to provide a building for these gifts. It opened just in time for President Garfield's inaugural ball in 1881. Exhibits are many and varied.

There is a 42-foot model sloop-of-war, Antietam and a Baldwin Locomotive. There are displays of jewelry, swords, clothing, buggies, guns, etc., all reflecting how it was in the 1800's. The building is located at 900 Jefferson Dr. S.W.

❸ ENID A. HAUPT GARDEN

There are Saucer Magnolias, hybrid tea roses and a Victorian embroidery parterre in this 4-acre park like area. The garden sits over the new underground museum, research and education complex and between the Castle, Freer Gallery, and the Arts and Industries Building. The main entrance is on Independence Avenue; however, it can also be reached on Jefferson Drive on the east and west sides of the Castle.

❹ FREER GALLERY OF ART

Freer Gallery, at Jefferson Drive and 12th Street, houses one of the world's finest collections of Oriental Art. Designed in the style of a Florentine renaissance palazzo, it has 2 rooms set aside for the work of James McNeill Whistler, a friend of the museum's founder, Charles Lang Freer. Freer was a multi-millionaire railroad car manufacturer who donated so much Oriental and American art that only about 8% of the 26,000 some items can be displayed at any one time. In addition to the Oriental and American art, there are art pieces from India, Iran, Egypt and Syria. A highlight of the museum is the Peacock Room designed entirely by James M. Whistler.

⑤ HIRSHHORN MUSEUM AND SCULPTURE GARDEN

Joseph Hirshhorn was a Latvian immigrant who made his fortune from uranium mines. He had purchased great quantities of art—over 4,000 paintings and 2,000 sculptures. He gave all of them to the United States as a gift. The museum proudly displays the largest public collection (in the United States) of sculpture by Henry Moore. A large collection of work by abstract expressionists from the 40's and 50's such as Pollack and de Kooning are represented here. Surrealist works by Salvador Dali and Tannguy share this building with sculptures of renowned artists such as Rodin, Moore, Nevelson, Cornell and di Suvero. The museum, at Independence Avenue and 7th streets, opened in 1974. Tours on any subject relevant to the museum may be arranged through the Education Department at 357-3235. The sculpture garden is open throughout the year from 7:30am-dusk.

⑥ NATIONAL AIR AND SPACE MUSEUM

Known as one of the most popular museums in the world, this huge building, at Independence Avenue and 6th streets, has 23 galleries devoted to the conquest of air and space travel. There are slide shows, movies of the space shuttle and flight pioneers, how-to-fly training school and hands-on learning devices for all ages.

Two must-sees are the Wright brother's Kitty Hawk Flyer and Lindbergh's Spirit of St. Louis. A model of the carrier, U.S.S. Enterprise are on the second floor, as well as the Albert Einstein Planetarium. Two exhibits are Looking at Earth, a view of the earth from balloons and satellites, and Computers in Aerospace, featuring technology of the future.

There is also a Paul E. Garber Facility in Suitland, Maryland which is open to the public.
Information 202-357-1400.
http://www.nasm.edu

❼ NATIONAL MUSEUM OF AFRICAN ART

Opened in 1987 at 950 Independence Avenue, on the National Mall, this museum displays a magnificent collection of over 6,000 objects of African art. One of the most outstanding pieces is a massive wood-carved door from the Yoruba King's palace at Ikere, Nigeria. On it are carved in relief 31 figures of people. As well as exhibition halls, this museum has classrooms, offices for scholars, an art research library and photograph archive.

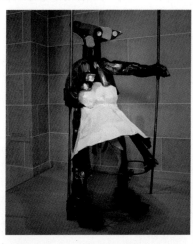

❽ NATIONAL MUSEUM OF AMERICAN HISTORY

This exciting museum is a storehouse of the accomplishments in science, technology, communications, politics, defense and home life of the American people. The main building is at 14th street and Constitution Avenue. Some of the wonderful things you can see here are a sampling of the gowns worn by our first Ladies, Alexander Graham Bell's first telephone, Thomas Edison's Light bulb, Eli Whitney's cotton gin, the desk used by Thomas Jefferson to draft the Declaration of Independence, and the original Star-Spangled Banner which inspired Francis Scott Key. Archie Bunker's chair and Mohammed Ali's boxing gloves remind us of more recent history.

The Centennial Exhibit in the Arts and Industries Building is actually part of this museum. School and adult tours are available from October through May.

Information 202-357-1481.

⑨ NATIONAL MUSEUM OF NATURAL HISTORY

The enormity of this museum at 10th and Constitution Avenue can be overwhelming but well worth several hours of time to see the wonderful exhibits displayed here. You don't want to miss the dazzling 45.5 carat Hope Diamond in the Hall of Gems or the animals ranging from a 360-million-year-old fossilized fish, a 90-foot giant squid, a stuffed 8-ton elephant and an 850-pound Bengal Tiger. One room, the Discovery Room, is of special interest for children because of its hands-on study. A special treat is a dress-up corner where kids can try on costumes from all over the world. The Insect Zoo can be fascinating and fun for kids of all ages. Also popular with children is the dinosaur exhibit.

⑩ S. DILLON RIPLEY CENTER

The center was named for the 8th secretary of the Smithsonian. It houses administrative offices for the Smithsonian Institution Travelling Exhibition Service, Resident and National Associate Programs, and the International Gallery. The International Center sponsors exhibitions, seminars, films, lectures and other public programs in the International Gallery. It is at 1100 Jefferson Drive S.W. near the Castle.

⑪ SMITHSONIAN INSTITUTION BUILDING (THE CASTLE)

This is the original building of the institution, at 1000 Jefferson Drive S.W. Designed by James Renwick Jr., it opened in 1855 and now houses administrative offices, the Woodrow Wilson International Center for Scholars and the Visitor Information Center.

Interesting to note is that the man who provided for the establishment, an Englishman named James Smithson, never visited the United States. His desire was to have a place "for the increase and diffusion of knowledge among men". His crypt is located here.

⑫ ANACOSTIA MUSEUM

At 1901 Fort Place S.E., this museum focuses on African-American history and community-related exhibitions, education and interpretive programs. Exhibitions have included Black aviators, the Harlem Renaissance and pioneering educator Anna Cooper. Hours 10:00am-5:00pm daily.

⑬ NATIONAL MUSEUM OF AMERICAN ART

33,000 works including paintings, sculptures, graphics, folk art, and photographs are displayed in this museum. Artists represented include Thomas H. Benton, Albert Bierstadt, Winslow Homer, Albert Ryder, George Catlin, Thomas Eakins and Robert Rauschenberg. The main museum, at 8th and G streets N.W., is in the same building as the National Portrait Gallery. The museum features the site of President Lincoln's 2nd inaugural reception and panoramic views of the American West by Thomas Moran. The Archives of American Art is also contained here. There is also the Barney Studio House located at 2306 Massachusetts Avenue N.W. which is open for tours. Appointments are necessary for the Barney Studio House tour. Information 202-357-3111.
Hours 10:00am-5:30pm daily.

The Paintings of Charles Burchfield

⑭ NATIONAL POSTAL MUSEUM

This museum is dedicated to the history of the U.S. Postal Service and philately. There are many exhibits and educational programs, including more thatn 30 audiovisual and interactive areas. Exhibits include Pony Express, "Binding The Nation" and "Taking to the Air". There is a library and research center. It is located across from Union Station. Hours 10am-5:30pm except Christmas.

Information 202-633-9380.

⑮ NATIONAL PORTRAIT GALLERY

Portraits of more than 700 Americans who contributed to the Nation's political, military, scientific, and cultural development are displayed here. The Gallery shares the old Patent Office Building with the National

Museum of American Art near the White House. The Portrait Gallery features the Hall of Presidents, the Time Magazine Cover Collection, Jo Davidson sculpture, and portrait of Mary Cassatt by Edgar Degas. Hours 10:00am-5:30pm daily.

⑯ NATIONAL ZOOLOGICALPARK

This spacious 165 acre zoo, representing over 3,000 animals and 500 species, was established in 1890 for the purpose of preserving some of the animal life in North America that was threatened with extinction. Outstanding features of the zoo are the 1.5-acre lion-tiger exhibit, the Great Ape House, the 90-foot Great Flight Cage and the Reptile House. This is the home of the panda, Hsing-Hsing, gift to the United States from the Peoples Republic of China in 1972. He is the only giant panda in the United States. The feeding times for the panda are 11:00 a.m. and 3:00 p.m. Hours (Sept. 16 - April 30) grounds: 8:00am-6:00pm; buildings: 9:00am-4:30pm (May 1 - Sept. 15) grounds: 8:00am-8:00pm; buildings: 9:00am-6:00pm.
The main entrance to the Zoo is located at the 3000 block of Connecticut Avenue.

⑰ RENWICK GALLERY

This building at Pennsylvania Avenue and 17th street N.W. was designed by architect James Renwick in 1859 and completed in 1874.

The building housed Washington's first private art museum. It now houses changing exhibitions of American craft artists of the 20th century. It features a Grand Salon, Octagon Room, and sales exhibitions of crafts in the museum shop. The main rooms are furnished in the style of the late 19th century. Hours 10:00am-5:30pm daily.
Information 202-357-2531.

⓲ NATIONAL GALLERY OF ART

The man who designed the Jefferson Memorial, John Russel Pope, also designed the beautiful white marble neo-classic building that opened in 1941. Funds were donated by Andrew Mellon, a philanthropist, who served as Secretary of the Treasury under Presidents Harding, Coolidge and Hoover. In 1978, an East Building was opened. They are connected by a plaza and underground concourse. The National Gallery of Art has the distinction of owning the only painting in America by Leonardo da Vinci, and it has the only set of portraits by Gilbert Stuart of the first five presidents of the United States. The West Building has a wonderful collection of French impressionist and post-impressionist art. A room full of paintings by Picasso is in the East building. Both buildings of the Gallery are located on the Mall at 6th and Constitution Avenue. Hours are Monday through Saturday 10:00am - 5:00pm; Sunday noon-9:00pm.
Closed Christmas Day and New Year's Day.
Information 202-737-4215.

⓳ NATIONAL GALLERY OF ART SCULPTURE GARDEN

The National Gallery of Art Sculpture Garden is scheduled to open the fall of 1998 as a donation from the Morris & Gwendolyn Cafritz Foundation, located across from the National Archives. There will be a variety of sculptures.
Information 202-842-6353.

⑳ JOHN F. KENNEDY CENTER FOR THE PERFORMING ARTS

The center of Washington D.C.'s cultural life is the John F. Kennedy Center for the Performing Arts. Opened in 1971, it is Washington D.C.'s official memorial to the late President. Gifts from many countries are incorporated into the structure such as the chandeliers in the Concert Hall that were a gift from Norway and the gold silk stage curtain in the Opera House from Japan.

The Center houses six theaters; the Opera House, the Concert Hall, the Eisenhower Theater, the Terrace Theater, the Theater Lab, and the American Film Institute Theater. The theaters range in seating capacity from 120 to 2,759. Performances of the finest in opera, dance, music, theater and film bring to Washington D.C. a new excellence in cultur-al events. The Center provides performances by presenting companies, acting as producer or coproducer, choosing outside attractions, supporting all concerts of the National Symphony Orchestra, leasing its halls to associated organizations on an ongoing basis, and leasing its halls to outside groups. The Performing Arts Library, a joint facility with the Library of Congress is housed in the Center. The Kennedy Center offers several public services to ensure that many people can enjoy the performing arts. Ticket Sales 202-857-0900, Handicapped Assistance 202-254-3774, Lost and Found 202-254-3676, Roof Terrace Restaurant 202-833-8870. Public Relations 202-254-3696. http://www.kennedy-center.org

3

TOUR 3: The Mall
1.) Washington Monument, 2.) Constitution Gardens, 3.) U.S. Holocaust Memorial Museum, 4.) Bureau of Printing and Engraving, 5.) Jefferson Memorial, 6.) Franklin Delano Roosevelt Memorial, 7.) Lincoln Memorial, 8.) Vietnam Veterans Memorial,

9.) Korean War Memorial.
Information: 202-426-6841: http://www.nps.gov/parklists/dc.html

❶ WASHINGTON MONUMENT

The Washington Monument is the most prominent and visible structure on the skyline of the nation's capital, jutting 555 feet into the air. There are 898 steps to the top. No one can use the steps now but arrangements can be made for the walking trip down. A 70 second elevator ride to the 500 foot level offers a magnificent view of the city and beyond into Maryland and Virginia. About 1/2 of the way up, the stone changes color. During the Civil War construction was halted and when it resumed the marble used was slightly different in hue even though it came from the same quarry. The Washington National Monument Society was organized in 1833 to erect the Monument; however, the cornerstone was not laid until 1848 and it was not open to the public until 1888. Tickets now avoid the long lines for the elevator ride up, so be patient as only 25 people may go at a time. The elevator was replaced in 1998. Once up, you may stay as long as you wish. The monument is open from 9:00am-5:00pm daily.
Information 202-426-6841.
http://www.nps.gov/wamo

❷ CONSTITUTION GARDENS

Along the tidal basin also between the Jefferson Memorial and the Lincoln Memorial is a collection of gardens as well as 60 statues and historical monuments.
http://www.nps.gov/coga

❸ U.S. HOLOCAUST MEMORIAL MUSEUM

The U.S. Holocaust Memorial Museum features exhibits and displays of the Holocaust in Nazi Germany. It opened in 1993. Of particular interest are the Wexner Learning Center-a computerized, hands-on learning experience; and Daniel's story, an exhibit concerning one boy's

experience with the Death Camps. There are also a research institute, a survivor's archive/registry, public programs and lectures. The museum is located at 14th Street and Independence Avenue S.W. and is open every day except Christmas and Yom Kippur.
Information 202-488-0400.
http://www.ushmm.org

❹ BUREAU OF ENGRAVING AND PRINTING

The Bureau is responsible for printing any official paper that carries a monetary value such as postage stamps, money and food stamps. Here you can observe the intricate process involved in producing 7,000 sheets of bills every hour. There are 65 separate steps in the production of paper money including intaglio printing, siderography, plate making, and the actual printing, examining, and over- printing. Security is tight and photography is forbidden. The Bureau began in 1862 with the separation and sealing of $1.00 and $2.00 bills which had been printed by private bank note companies. Since 1877 all United States Currency has been printed in the Bureau. Tours are conducted from 9:00am-2:00pm Monday through Friday.

http://www.access.gpo.gov

❺ JEFFERSON MEMORIAL

This distinctive domed building houses a 19 foot high statue of our third President of the United States and the author of the Declaration of Independence. Domes on buildings were favored by Jefferson, himself an architect. Above the entrance, which faces the Tidal Basin, is a sculpture which depicts Jefferson standing before the committee appointed by the Continental Congress to write the Declaration of Independence. There are four panels on the interior walls which are engraved with writings of the third President. Surrounding the Memorial are the famous Oriental Cherry Trees. When they are in bloom in early April, thousands of visitors come to see the beautiful blossoms during the "Cherry Blossom Festival". The memorial is open at all times.
Information 202-426-6841.
http://www.nps.gov/thje

❻ FRANKLIN DELANO ROOSEVELT MEMORIAL

Located between the Jefferson Memorial and the Lincoln Memorial, this Memorial is dedicated to President Franklin Delano Roosevelt, who saw the United States through the Great Depression and World War II. It contains sculptures and inscriptions reminiscent of all four terms of office. The sculptor of the seated president and pet Fala is Neil Estern, the inscriptionist is John Benson. It was dedicated in 1997 and is open to the public every day except Christmas.
http://www.nps.gov/fdrm

❼ LINCOLN MEMORIAL

This inspiring tribute to our 16th president provides a breathtaking view of the Capitol. A 19 foot white Georgian marble figure of Lincoln sits and gazes down the Mall toward the Washington Monument.

Flanking the statue on one side is the Gettysburg Address and on the other side is the Second Inaugural Address. Above these inscriptions are murals painted by Jules Guerin. The memorial has gone through fits and starts. The first attempt to erect a monument to Lincoln in Washington came in 1867. There were subsequent efforts but only in 1911 did Congress pass legislation which led to the memorial. The cornerstone was laid in 1915 and it was completed in 1922. The design for this classic greek structure was submitted by Henry Bacon. The statue was designed by Daniel Chester French and carved by the Piccirilli brothers in their New York Studio. The memorial is open at all times; however, a ranger is in attendance from 8:00am-midnight daily except Christmas Day.

Information 202-426-6841.

http://www.nps.gov/linc

❽ VIETNAM VETERANS MEMORIAL

The 58,132 men and women who died in service related to the Vietnam War are honored here. The Memorial, on the National Mall near the Lincoln Memorial, was dedicated in 1982. It is not the traditional white marble tribute but consists of 2 highly polished granite walls that meet to form a V. On the walls are inscribed all 58,132 names, which are placed in chronological order of the date of casualty. Each name is accompanied by either a diamond or cross. The diamond is for those confirmed dead; whereas, the cross is for those approximately 1300 persons who are missing or prisoners of war. If a person returns, a circle is inscribed around the cross. The 2 walls are angled so as to enfold the Washington Monument and the Lincoln Memorial in a symbolic embrace linking past to present. A part of this memorial is a separate three soldier sculpture. All monies for this memorial came from private donations. The Memorial is open from 8:00am-midnight year round.

Information 202-426-6841.

http://www.nps.gov/vive

⑨ KOREAN WAR MEMORIAL

Located at the foot of the Lincoln Memorial, this Memorial is dedicated to those who served and died in the Korean War. The memorial consists of bronze statues of soldiers in full battle dress, all marching towards the United States Flag. There is also a mural at the memorial. The sculptor is Frank Gaylord III, with Louis Nelson Associates as Muralists. The architects/designers of the Memorial are Cooper-Lecky, Inc.

http://www.nps.gov/kwvm

4

TOUR 4: White House Area

1.) St. John's Church, 2.) Department of Interior Building and Museum, 3.) Treasury Department, 4.) National Aquarium, 5.) White House, 6.) Decatur House Museum, 7.) Blair-Lee House, 8.) Renwick Gallery, 9.) Executive Office Building, 10.) Corcoran Gallery of Art, 11.) American Red

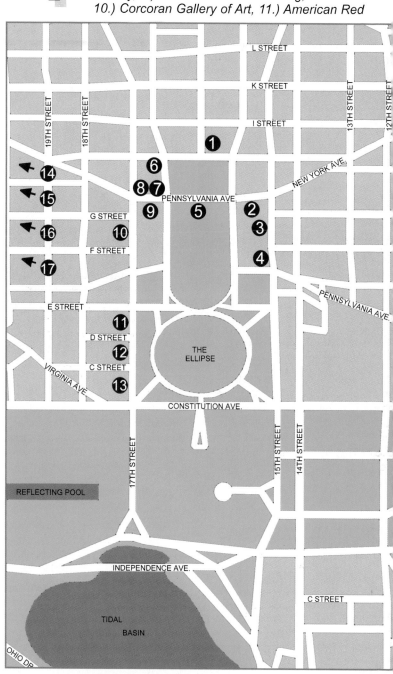

Cross, National Headquarters, 12.) Continental Hall, DAR Museum, 3.) Organization of American States Building, 14.) Watergate Complex, 15.) George Washington University, 16.) National Geographic Society Headquarters, 17.) Kennedy Center.

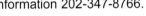

❶ ST. JOHN'S CHURCH

This church was built in 1815 by Benjamin Henry Latrobe. Every president since Madison has at one time or another attended services here. The church is open from 8:00am-4:00pm daily. Tours are given following the 11:00am service on Sunday and may be arranged at other times by calling the Parish Office.
Information 202-347-8766.

❷ DEPARTMENT OF INTERIOR BUILDING AND MUSEUM

The department of interior building houses four attractions which are open to the public: The U.S. Geological Survey Earth Sciences Information Center, The National Park Service Information Center, The Department of Interior Museum, and The Indian Craft Shop. A photo I.D. is necessary for each visitor for admission to the last three places. http://www.doi.gov

U.S. Geological Survey Earth Sciences Information Center
This Field location of the National U.S.G.S. center in Reston, Va. publishes topographic maps of the U.S., Geologic maps and book reports, and basic information on water resources of the country. It is open to the public 8:00am-4:00pm Monday-Friday.

National Park Service Information Center
This office contains brochures and information about all the national parks and reservations throughout the United States. This is perfect for planning not only visits to the many parks in the Washington D.C. area, but possibly next year's vacation to some other area of the country. http://www.nps.gov

Department of Interior Museum
In order to present the Department's history and objectives, then Secretary Harold L. Ickes included a museum in the Interior building. The museum opened on March 8, 1938. It maintains the 1930's flavor to its exhibits which include survey equipment, preserved animal specimens, native artifacts, a description of mapping techniques, and dioramas depicting various activities of the Department in the field.

The museum is open from 8:00am-4:00pm Monday-Friday. Information 202-343-2743. http://www.doi.gov

Indian Craft Shop

This shop, started in 1938 as a WPA project under President Roosevelt, features native American and Alaskan artwork, pottery, jewelry, sand paintings, kachinas, fetishes and rugs all for sale. Hours are from 8:30am-4:30pm Monday-Friday. Information 202-208-4056. http://www.atiin.com/iaca

❸ TREASURY DEPARTMENT

The entire Treasury Building covers 5 acres. It is built in a Greek Revival style with walls of granite. The existing building is the third one built on the site. The previous two were destroyed by fire. All the area bounding the building is Washington's financial district. There are no public tours of the main building. A reproduction of the Liberty Bell is on permanent display on the west side.

❹ NATIONAL AQUARIUM

The Department of Commerce Building that stretches over a block long houses the aquarium. This aquarium is the oldest in the country being founded in 1873. There are 65 exhibits including a shark tank, a piranha tank, and a sea turtle tank. Children will enjoy the "touch tank". It gives hands-on experience with marine life.

Also visit the mini-theater. There is a shark feeding

every Monday, Wednesday, an Saturday at 2:00pm as well as piranha feeding every Tuesda Thursday, and Sunday, also a 2:00. The aquarium is ope 9:00am - 5:00pm daily excep Christmas. Tours are availabl for the hearing impaired wit advance notice 202-377-2826 For recorded information ca 202-377-2825.

⑤ WHITE HOUSE

1600 Pennsylvania Avenue is perhaps the best known address in the Nation. George Washington was our only president not to live in the White House. It opened in 1800 with President John Adams as its first resident. It nearly burned to the ground in 1814

when British troops set it afire. In 1948, under Truman's administration, it was virtually rebuilt around a steel frame. Five of the 132 rooms are open to the public. They are the East Room, the Blue Room, the Red Room, and the State Dining Room. The East Room is the site of the Presidential news conferences, it has been used for four First Family weddings, (Nellie Grant, Alice Roosevelt, Jessie Wilson and Lynda Bird

Johnson) and the funerals of six Presidents, (Harrison, Taylor, Lincoln, Harding, Franklin Roosevelt and Kennedy). In the adjoining Executive Offices, the President transacts his duties; holds Cabinet meetings; receives members of Congress, government officials and foreign dignitaries. Tours are available from 10:00am-noon Tuesday through Saturday from Labor Day to Memorial Day, but it can be closed to the public for official functions with little notice. The ticket booth opens at 8:00am. East Executive Park is open to the public from 5:00am-11:00pm.
Information 202-755-7798.
http://www.whitehouse.gov;
http://www.nps.gov/whho;
http://www.whitehousehistory.org.

⑥ DECATUR HOUSE MUSEUM

This museum at 748 Jackson Place has the artifacts for the Federal period (1820) and the Victorian period (1880) in American history. Commodore Stephen Decatur settled here after fighting pirates in the Barbary Wars and the British in the War of 1812. Both Henry Clay and Martin Van Buren lived here and aspired to the Presidency. In 1871 the Edward F. Beale family purchased the house. It stayed with the Beale family until 1956 when Mrs. Marie Oge Beale

bequeathed it to the National Trust for Historic Preservation. The Decatur House has been and continues to be a center for Washington social events. In addition there are special events which include a quilt show in February, a market-place for 19th century crafts in November, and walking tours of historic Lafayette park. Guided tours available weekdays 10:00am-1:30pm, weekends noon-3:30pm.
Information 202-842-0920
http://www.nthhp.org

❼ BLAIR-LEE HOUSE

Built in 1824, Blair House was the home of Francis Preston Blair, editor of the Globe (a predecessor of today's Washington Post), and also of his son Montgomery Blair, attorney for Dred Scott and Postmaster General under President Lincoln. Lee House, just next door, was erected in 1858. Admiral Samuel Phillips Lee, who commanded the North Atlantic Blockading Squadron during the Civil War lived here. Also Lee House was the first headquarters of the Reserve Officers Association from 1924 to 1938. The two houses were joined in 1943. During reconstruction of the White House from 1948-1952, President Truman and his family occupied the Blair House. While living here, an attempt on his life by Puerto Rican fanatics resulted in the death of a White House guard.

❽ RENWICK GALLERY
See Tour 2: Smithsonian

OLD EXECUTIVE OFFICE BUILDING

The Executive Office Building was formerly the headquarters for the Department of State, War, and Navy. It is now part of the executive office of the President. Tours are available on Saturday mornings from 9:00am-noon by reservation only. Reservations may be made between 9:00am-noon, Monday through Friday at 202-395-5895 or 202-395-5896. When calling have available the date of birth and social security number for each visitor.

CORCORAN GALLERY OF ART

William Wilson Corcoran founded this museum in 1869 to house his private collection. It is the oldest and largest private art museum in Washington D.C. In 1897, It was moved to its present location from where the Renwick Gallery is now. The famous Stuart portrait of George Washington that is reproduced on one dollar bills hangs here. Fine American art is represented by Gilbert Stuart, John Singer Sargent, Mary Cassatt, Josef Albers and Rembrandt Peale. The European collection includes works by notables such as Gaensborough, Constable and J.M. Turner. Information 202-639-1700 http://www.corcoran.org

AMERICAN RED CROSS, NATIONAL HEADQUARTERS

This marble Corinthian style building was built as a memorial to the women who helped the sick and wounded during the Civil War. It was begun in 1915 and completed in 1917. Contained in it are displays and exhibits of the Red Cross programs as well as paintings and sculptures. In the Board of Governors Room is a suite of Tiffany windows which is the largest outside of a church in the United States. In the garden is a monument to Jane A. Delano, the founder of the Red Cross Nursing Program. Hours 8:30am-4:00pm Monday through Friday. http://www.red-cross.org

⑫ CONTINENTAL HALL, DAR MUSEUM

The three buildings, located at 17th and D streets N.W., of the Daughters of the American Revolution include Continental Hall, designed by Edward P. Casey and completed in 1910; The administration Building; and Constitution Hall, designed by John Russel Pope. The great auditorium seats 4,000 persons and is used as Washington's cultural center. Lecturers, explorers, scientists, and speakers are heard by capacity audiences. The DAR Genealogical Library houses thousands of volumes used in tracing family connections. The huge library occupies the converted old auditorium in Memorial Continental Hall. The DAR museum consists of 3 period rooms that reflect th diversity of craftsmanship in pre industrial America. Collection focus on decorative arts mad or used in America prior to 186 including furniture, silver, glass ceramics, textiles, and pain ings. In addition to the perma nent period rooms there is changing exhibition schedule Museum hours 8:30am-4:00pr Monday through Friday 1:00pm-5:00pm Sunday, close Saturday and holidays. Als closed during April.
Information 202-879-3254.
http://www.dar.org/contintenta hall.html;
http://www.dar.org/constitutio hall.html

⑬ ORGANIZATION OF AMERICAN STATES BUILDINC

This landmark next to Contintental Hall features a Tropical Patio, Hall of the Americas and an Aztec Garden. Some conference rooms are occasionally open to the public. There are free guided tours Monday-Friday from 9:30am to 3:30pm. Reservations are required. Information and reser vations 202-458-3751.
http://www.oas.org

⑭ WATERGATE COMPLEX

This exclusive area of expensive shops, apartments and offices is where the break-in of the Democratic National Committee offices eventually led to President Nixon's resignation. The 29 shops include fine restaurants, which due to the proximity to the Kennedy Center, offer an excellent place for dinner before the show. The hotel offers good concierge services from 7:00am-11:00pm daily. It boasts completely refurbished rooms on all levels. Information 202-965-2300. http://www.travel2000.com/c/united_s/district/washinton.udc/wg3.htm

⓯ GEORGE WASHINGTON UNIVERSITY

George Washington University, 2029 H Street, N.W. was founded in 1821, as the result of a wish of George Washington that such a university might be established in the Nation's Capital, "to which the youth of fortune and talents from all parts thereof might be sent for the completion of their education in all the branches of polite literature; in arts and sciences, in acquiring knowledge in the principles of politics and good government." From a small beginning with 39 students, the University's enrollment has grown to a total of more than 19,000 today. Undergraduate and graduate work is offered in the Arts and Sciences, Law, Medicine, Government, Education, Engineering. There are three libraries on campus. A variety of performances are open to the public in the Lisner Auditorium. Information 202-994-6800. http://www.gwu.edu

⓰ NATIONAL GEOGRAPHIC SOCIETY HEADQUARTERS

National Geographic Society, 17th and M Street, N.W. As the headquarters of the National Geographic Society, largest scientific and educational organization in the world, it is here all the Society's exploration projects are planned and the National Geographic Magazine is prepared. In Explorers Hall are mementos and trophies from famed Geographic expeditions. The Library contains thousands of volumes on every phase of geography. One of the permanent exhibits is the world's largest globe— 11 feet from pole to pole. Founded in 1888, the Society now has a membership of over 3,900,000. http://www.nationalgeographic.com

⓱ KENNEDY CENTER

See Tour 2: Smithsonian

54

5 TOUR 5: Downtown Area

1.) National Archives, 2.) U.S. Navy Memorial, 3.) Post Office Pavilion, 4.) F.B.I. Headquarters, 5.) Martin Luther King Library, 6.) Ford's Theater/Lincoln Museum, 7.) National Museum of American Art, 8.) National Portrait Gallery.

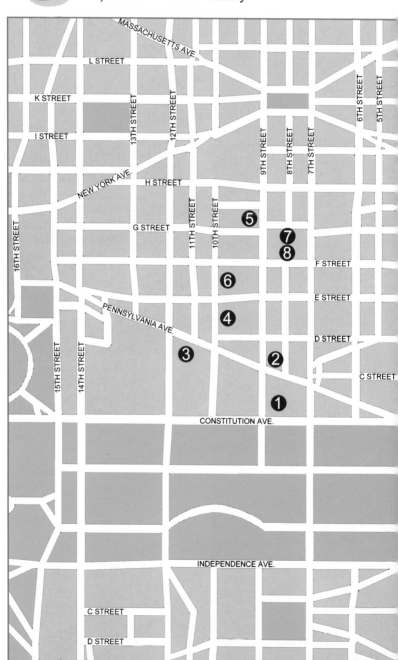

❶ NATIONAL ARCHIVES

The most important documents of U.S. History are displayed here. In special cases are the original Declaration of Independence, the Constitution, and Bill of Rights, and on indefinite loan is an original copy (one of only 15) of the Magna Charta. Hours are 4/1-Labor Day: 10am-9:30pm; Labor Day-3/31: 10am-5:30pm. Special Events include 9/17-Constitution Day, and 7/4-Independence Day. From the Pennsylvania Avenue access it is possible to do genealogical research or other research. An I.D. card is necessary for access to the material, but these can be obtained at the front desk. Tours are available for this section by appointment only. Call 523-3183. The Archives has one of the finest document restoration teams in the world. In addition to paper documents, the Archives holds over 7 million still photographs, some dating back to the Civil War, as well as motion pictures. New citizens of the United States are sworn in at the Rotunda on September 17th of each year(Constitution Day).

The genealogy section is open from 8:45am-9:45pm Monday through Saturday. The motion picture and still picture sections are only open 9:00am-5:00pm Monday through Friday. There are 14 branches of the National Archives across the country. Two additional ones are in the Washington D.C. metropolitan area: Suitland, Md. and Picket Street in Alexandria, Va. http://www.nana.gov

❷ U.S. NAVY MEMORIAL

This memorial, across Pennsylvania Avenue from the National Archives, features two masts and a statue of a sailor. It commemorates those Naval personnel who served the nation, who are serving now, and especially those who gave their lives in service to the country. http://www.lonesailor.org

❸ THE POST OFFICE PAVILION

This old building at 12th and Pennsylvania Avenue has been converted to a nice collection of shops, including several restaurants. It is built in the Richardsonian Romanesque style of architecture. There is a glass elevator which gives a nice view of the pavilion in the clock tower. The top of the clock tower is open to the public for a breathtaking view of Washington. Surprisingly this building was scheduled for demolition in 1971, but several groups called for its restoration. It now houses the National Endowment for the Arts and the National Endowment for the Humanities. The tower and shops are open 10:00am-6:00pm daily. Restaurants are open later for dinner.
Information: 202-523-5691.
http://www.nps.gov/opot

❹ F.B.I. HEADQUARTERS

Free 60 minute tours provide a glimpse of what the F.B.I. is about. A special area honors J. Edgar Hoover, the director of the F.B.I. from 1924-1972. Also shown on the tour is the labs where current investigations are conducted, and a live firearms demonstration.

Tours are offered on a walk-in basis from 8:45am-4:15pm Monday-Friday except holidays. Scheduled tours may be arranged 6-8 weeks in advance by your Congressman. Security is tight so be prepared to have all bags inspected, and to go through a metal detector. http://www.fbi.gov

⑤ MARTIN LUTHER KING LIBRARY

Mies van de Rohe's building design gives added importance to this fine library. It features the Washingtonian section which specializes in information on the city from its beginnings to the present day. Other attractions are a bookstore, a Black Studies room, and "the Other Place"—a room with books for young adults.

Be sure to see Don Miller's mural located in the main lobby which depicts various scenes from Dr. King's life.

⑥ FORD'S THEATER/LINCOLN MUSEUM

Ford's Theater, where President Lincoln was assassinated on Good Friday, April 14, 1865, is restored to re-create the setting where this tragic event occurred. Periodic talks concerning the assassination are given by Park Rangers. Some language assistance is available.

Also, visit the Petersen House, where President Lincoln died. It also re-creates the setting for the historic event. John Wilkes Booth's exhibit is here as well. There is a bookstore in the House Where Lincoln Died open from 9:00am-4:30pm. The historic site is run by the U.S. Park Service and is open daily from 9:00am-5:00pm except December 25. The theater puts on a full schedule of plays, covering a wide range of American cultural and ethnic diversity.

The theater is closed to tours when rehearsals of matinees are in progress. These usually occur on Thursday, Saturday, and Sunday. Box office information 202-347-4833. Park Information 202-426-6924. Petersen House Information 202-426-6830. http://www.nps.gov/foth

⑦ NATIONAL MUSEUM OF AMERICAN ART
See Tour 2: Smithsonian

⑧ NATIONAL PORTRAIT GALLERY
See Tour 2: Smithsonian

TOUR 6: Georgetown
*1.) Art Galleries, 2.) Georgetown Park, 3.) Georgeto
University, 4.) C & O Canal, 5.) Washington Harbo
6.) Dunbarton Oaks*

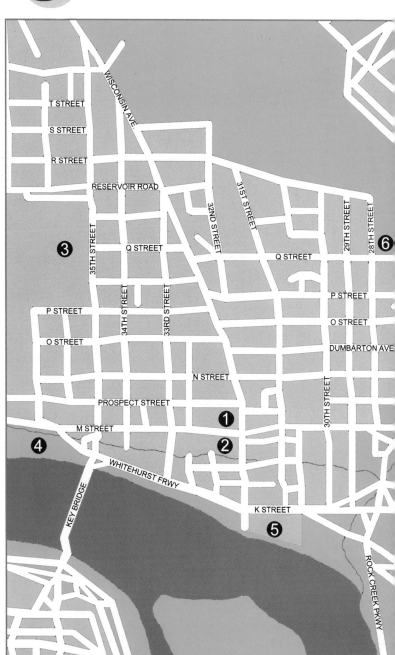

GEORGETOWN

Georgetown began as an Indian trading center. In 1789, the town was incorporated. This district boasts some of the most unique boutiques, shops, night spots, and varied range of restaurants.

❶ ART GALLERIES

There are dozens of art galleries scattered through Georgetown. They feature all varieties of art from paintings to sculpture, from Eastern to Modern. Some of the galleries include the Eastern Gallery (202-333-0183), The Atlantic Gallery of Georgetown (202-337-2299), The Moss Portfolio Ltd. (202-338-5598), Inner-Visions of Georgetown (202-342-6695), The Worthy Gallery (202-342-0101), Spectrum Gallery (202-333-0943), Gallery Lareuse (202-333-5704), Andreas Galleries (202-337-2000), Justine S. Mehlman Fine Art (202-337-8645), Fendrick Gallery (202-338-4544), The Old Print Gallery (202-965-1818), Circle Gallery (202-338-6455), Georgetown Gallery of Art (202-333-6308), Taggart & Jorgensen Gallery (202-298-7676), Washington Studio School Gallery (202-333-2663), Maurine Littleton Gallery (202-333-9307), Bishops Gallery (202-333-7701), Susan Conway Carroll Gallery (202-333-4082), and Animation Sensations (202-965-0199).

❷ GEORGETOWN PARK

This shopping mall contains over 100 shops on 4 levels including 5 art galleries and a museum room which gives the history of the site. The shops are open Monday-Friday 10:00am-9:00pm; Saturday 10:00am-7:00pm; Sunday noon-6:00. There is paid underground parking off of Wisconsin Avenue.

❸ GEORGETOWN UNIVERSITY

In 1789 Georgetown University was founded as the first Roman Catholic university in the U.S. The University has Schools in Arts and Sciences, Foreign Service, Languages and Linguistics, Business Administration, Nursing, Medicine, Dentistry, and Law. It boasts an enrollment of more than 11,000 students.
Information 202-687-3600.
http://data.georgetown.edu

❹ C & 0 CANAL

Some of the locks of the C & O Canal are located in Georgetown. They blend in with the character of the shops.

❺ WASHINGTON HARBOUR

A beautiful plaza on the Potomac is Washington Harbour. It is a complex of offices, restaurants, shops and apartments located on the north bank with a view of Key Bridge.

❻ DUNBARTON OAKS

Dunbarton Oaks in Georgetown is a 19th century mansion turned museum. It has a collection of Byzantine jewelry and pre-Columbian art.
The surrounding gardens are meticulously cared for. Tours are conducted on Tuesdays, Wednesdays, Thursdays, and Saturdays. Reservations are required.
Information 202-342-3212.

7

TOUR 7: Arlington
1.) Arlington National Cemetery, 2.) Custis Lee Mansion (Arlington House), 3.) Women in Military Memorial, 4.) Tomb of the Unknown Soldier, 5.) John F. Kennedy Grave, 6.) Arlington Memorial Amphitheater, 7.) Netherlands Carillon,

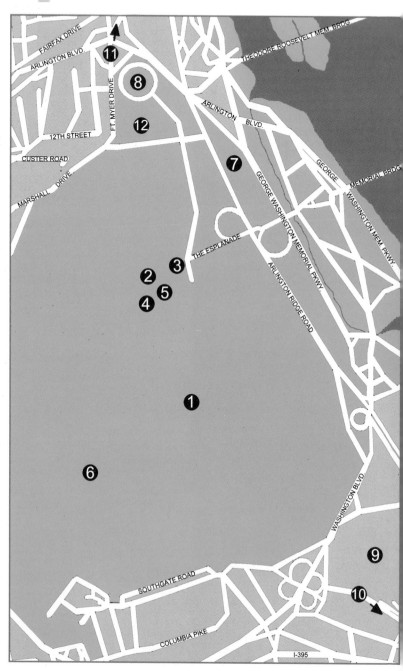

8.) *U.S. Marine Corps War Memorial,* 9.) *Pentagon,* 10.) *Ronald Reagan Washington National Airport,* 11.) *Newseum,* 12.) *Air Force Memorial*

❶ ARLINGTON NATIONAL CEMETERY

Over 1,000 acres of Virginia, just across the Potomac River from Washington D.C. is Arlington National Cemetery. Buried here are war heroes from the Revolutionary War to the Vietnam War, Presidents John F. Kennedy and William Howard Taft, Robert F. Kennedy, as well as notable ex-servicemen.

Pierre L'Enfant, Washington D.C.'s first city planner, is buried just south of the Custis Lee Mansion. There are memorials to the crew of the U.S.S. Maine, the Challenger Astronauts,and the servicemen of the Iranian Rescue Mission.

http://www.ourworld.com-puserve.com/homepages/michael_patterson_4

❷ CUSTIS LEE MANSION (ARLINGTON HOUSE)

The adopted son of George Washington, George Washington Parke Custis, built the Mansion on a hill on this former Lee estate in the early 1800's. His daughter, Mary, and her husband and military commander Robert E. Lee, lived here with their 7 children. During the Civil War, the general and his wife had to abandon the house. Wartime law allowed the Union to confiscate the property in 1864; however, General Lee was able to win it back in court. By that time, hun-

dreds of graves covered the hills. This was the beginning of Arlington Cemetery. The mansion was finally transferred to the National Park Service in 1933, and declared a memorial to Robert E. Lee in 1955.

Arlington House is open 9:30am-6:00pm April through September; 9:30am-4:30pm October through March.

Group tours are available by appointment.

❸ WOMEN IN MILITARY SERVICE MEMORIAL

This memorial is dedicated to the roughly 2 million women who serve and have served in all branches of the armed services since 1776. The memorial contains a Hall of Honor; a computerized Register; exhibits showcasing artifacts, texts, and memorable images donated by servicewomen. There is also a theatre where some films are played and also a small gift shop. Hours: 8am-5pm October to March; 8am-7pm April to September. Phone 1-800-222-2294. http://www.wimsa.org

❹ TOMB OF THE UNKNOWNS

Day and night, a lone sentry paces back and forth before this tomb where the Unknown Soldiers of World War I, World War II, the Korean Conflict, and the Vietnam Conflict lie. The inscription reads, "Here rests in honored glory an American Soldier, known but to God". The sentry is specially chosen from the first Battle Group, third Infantry, part of the Military District of Washington command.

❺ GRAVE OF JOHN F. KENNEDY

Here burns the eternal flame that memorializes our 35th President of the United States, John F. Kennedy and his wife Jacqueline.

❻ ARLINGTON MEMORIAL AMPHITHEATER

Patriotic assemblies gather here on special occasions such as Memorial Day, Veterans Day, and Easter Sunrise. The outer rim is lined with a colonnade and boxes. The seating capacity is 5,000. No funerals are held here.

❼ NETHERLANDS CARILLON

Her Majesty Queen Juliana of the Netherlands presented a small silver bell to President Truman in 1952 to symbolize the Carillon that the Netherlands would give to the United States. Erected in 1960, this set of 49 bells has represented the friendship between the two nations. A Carillon is an instrument comprising at least two octaves of fixed, cup-shaped bells arranged in chromatic series and so tuned as to produce concordant harmony.

Concerts are given on Saturdays from April through September. April, May, and September recitals are from 2:00-4:00pm; June, July, and August recitals are from 6:30-8:30pm. During the concerts guests are permitted to climb the tower to see the carillon played and chat with the carillonneur between selections. http://www.co.arlington.va.us/acvs/netherld.htm

❽ U.S. MARINE CORPS WAR MEMORIAL

The 78 foot high bronze sculpture of five Marines and a Navy hospital corpsman raising the flag on the top of an extinct volcano in Japan is a tribute to all marines who gave their lives for the United States sinc 1775. President Kennedy, i 1961, decreed that a cloth fla fly from the Memorial's flagpol 24 hours a day.

❾ PENTAGON

The Pentagon is our U.S. Defense Department Headquarters. Here the secretaries of the Army, Navy, Air Force and Coast Guard have their offices. More than 23,000 people work here. There are five sides and 5 floors in this building with over 17 miles of corridors. It was completed in 1943 after 16 months of construction. Tours are offered Monday through Friday (except Federal Holidays) every ha hour from 9:30am to 3:30pm From October through April th 10:30am, 1:30pm, and 3:00pn tours are not offered. A 1: minute film is shown and a wall through certain hallways make: up the tour. The walk-through visits the Commander-in-Chie Corridor; Army, Air Force, and Navy Executive Corridors; Ai Force Art Collection; POW/MI/ Display; Army Past Chiefs o

Staff Corridor; Time-Life Art Collection; Hall of Heroes; Military Women's Corridor; and the Flag Corridor. In the Hall of Heroes, you will find the names of the 3,000 men and 1 woman who have received the Medal of

Honor. Note that visitors must undergo airport-like security checks before the tour begins. Also a photo I.D. is required for all visitors. Brochures are available in English, Spanish, French, German, and Japanese.
Information 703-695-1776.
http://www.dcmilitary.com

⑩ RONALD REAGAN WASHINGTON NATIONAL AIRPORT

Between Alexandria, Va. and Washington, D.C. is the Ronald Reagan Washington National Airport. It is built on reclaimed mud flats and marshes of the Potomac River. It is owned by the U.S. Government and operated by the Metopolitan Washington Airports Authority.

In 1997 the new terminal opened with a beautiful arcade of shops, on February 6,1998 it was renamed from Washington National Airport to honor former President Ronald Reagan. http://www.met-washairports.com

⑪ NEWSEUM

The Newseum is the only interactive museum of news. Located in Arlington, Va. The Newseum takes visitors behind the scenes to see and experience how and why news is made. Visitors can be reporters or television newscasters, relive the great news stories of all times, and see today's news as it happens on a block-long video news wall. Hours: Wed-Sun 10:00am-5:00pm; closed Thanksgiving, Christmas, and New Year's Day. Freedom Park is open daily. Information 703-284-3544. http://www.newseum.org

⑫ AIR FORCE MEMORIAL

Proposed for construction near the Iwo Jima, Marine Corps War Memorial is the Air Force Memorial. Information 703-247-5808. http://www.air-forcememorial.org

8

TOUR 8: Alexandria and Mount Vernon

1.) Ramsay House, 2.) Stabler-Leadbeater Apothecary Shop, 3.) Old Presbyterian Meeting House, 4.) The Athenaeum, 5.) The Torpedo Facto Art Center, 6.) Carlyle House, 7.) Market Square/Ci

Hall, 8.) Gadsby's Tavern Museum, 9.) Boyhood Home of Robert E. Lee, 10.) Lee-Fendall House, 11.) Lloyd House, 12.) Christ Church, 13.) The Lyceum, 14.) Friendship Veterans Fire Engine Association, 15.) Black History Resource Center, 16.) Alexandria Waterfront Museum, 17.) George Washington Masonic Memorial, 18.) Fort Ward Museum and Historic Site, 19.) Washington's Grist Mill, 20.) Gunston Hall Plantation, 21.) Woodlawn Plantation and Frank Lloyd Wright's Pope-Leighey House, 22.) Mount Vernon

OLD TOWN ALEXANDRIA

Unless otherwise noted, all sites can be found on the web from http://ci.alexandria.va.us/oha;
http://www.oldtowncrier.com
Old town Alexandria is a unique experience with shops, historic sights and a view of the Potomac. Guided walking tours are offered starting at Ramsay House Monday through Saturday at 11:00am; Sunday, 2:00pm, April through November. Information 703-548-0100. The Admiral Tilp offers a view of Alexandria by boat. Tours run hourly from 11:00am-3:00pm Monday through Friday; hourly 10:00am-4:00pm Saturday and Sunday, May through Labor Day. Information 703-548-9000.

❶ RAMSAY HOUSE

This house was originally built in 1724 by William Ramsay, one of the city's founders, and its first postmaster. After Ramsay's death in 1785, the house changed hands many times and was put to various uses including a tavern, grocery store, rooming house and cigar factory. In 1956, the visitors Center was opened here.
Information 703-838-4200.

❷ STABLER-LEADBEATER APOTHECARY SHOP

This apothecary shop was in continuous operation from 1792 to 1933, during which powders and cosmetics were manufactured there. It now features exhibits of medical ware and hand blown glass containers. Information 703-836-3713.

❸ OLD PRESBYTERIAN MEETING HOUSE

This house was built in 1774 by Scotch-Irish pioneers. It served as a meeting place for patriots. The funeral sermons for George Washington were preached here. It is now an active church, and visitors are welcome.
Information 703-549-6670.

❹ THE ATHENAEUM

This building is built in the Greek Revival Architecture. The Northern Virginia Fine Arts Association features contemporary art shows here.
Closed during the summer.
Information 703-548-0035.

⑤ THE TORPEDO FACTORY ART CENTER

Built in 1918 as a torpedo factory, the weapons were manufactured here until 1946. After World War II, the building served as a repository for war records. In 1969, the City of Alexandria bought the building from the Federal Government. The Torpedo Factory now houses 84 studios and 4 galleries for the arts. Over 150 professional artists work, exhibit and sell their art. The types of art represented here include ceramics, enameling, etched crystal, textiles, jewelry, musical instruments, painting, photography, printmaking, sculpture, and stained glass. Open 7 days a week from 10:00am-5:00pm. There is also an archaeology museum here.
Information 703-838-4565.

⑥ CARLYLE HOUSE

John Carlyle, one of the founders of Alexandria, built this mansion in 1752. It became the headquarters for General Braddock upon his arrival in this country. It was here at a conference of Governors that plans were formulated to abolish Colonial Taxation. Guided tours are offered every half hour. Open Tuesday through Saturday 10:00am-5:00pm; Sunday noon-5:00pm; Closed Monday.
Information 703-549-2997.

⑦ MARKET SQUARE/CITY HALL

In 1749, an acre was reserved for a marketplace and town hall. The building has become schools, jails, whipping posts, private fire companies. In 1871 a U-shaped Victorian building was built with a central courtyard for a market. On Saturday mornings you can visit the oldest continuously operating market in the country.
Information 703-383-4000.

⑧ GADSBY'S TAVERN MUSEUM

This 2 story landmark, built in 1752, was the site of many historic events. It was Washington's headquarters while recruiting rangers for the campaign of 1754. The first celebration of the adoption of the Federal Constitution was held here in 1788. Mr. and Mrs. Washington often danced in the ballroom of the tavern. Today you may visit the fully restored buildings (two). A colonial style restaurant serves visitors in three of the tavern rooms. Hours: Tuesday through Saturday 10:00am-5:00pm; Sunday 1:00am-5:00pm. Information 703-838-4242.

⑨ BOYHOOD HOME OF ROBERT E. LEE

In this house Robert E. Lee spent most of his boyhood years. It is decorated with authentic period pieces. It was also where Mary Lee Fitzhugh married George Washington Parke Custis. Special events conducted here include Robert E. Lee's Birthday celebration in January, a reenactment of The Fitzhugh-Custis wedding in July, a reenactment of the formal visit of the Marquis de Lafayette in October, and an Alexandria Candlelight tour in December. The house is open Monday - Saturday 10:00am-4:00pm, Sunday noon-4:00pm. Guided tours are given. Information 703-548-8454

⑩ LEE-FENDALL HOUSE

This house was built in 1785 by Philip Fendall. It was frequented by his cousin "Light Horse Harry" Lee and friend George Washington. It was home to 37 of the Lees from 1785-1903. The museum now exhibits Lee family furnishings, family records, archeological and historic research, a study of 19th century life, and a collection of doll houses. Guided tours are offered. Open 10:00am-3:45pm Tuesday through Saturday, noon-3:45pm Sunday.

⑪ LLOYD HOUSE

Built in 1797 by John Wise, this house is an example of late Georgian Architecture. In the early 1800's James Marshall, brother of Chief Justice John Marshall, lived here. It is now a part of the Alexandria Library, and houses a collection of rare books, records and documents concerning the city. The first floor is a museum containing books and papers contained in the original 1794 subscription library. Open Monday-Saturday 9:00am-5:00pm.
Information 703-838-4577.

⑫ CHRIST CHURCH

Christ Church was the first Episcopal Church in Alexandria. Designed by James Wren, it is a typical example of pre-Revolutionary church architecture of the Georgian period. Mr. and Mrs. George Washington worshipped here and Robert E. Lee was confirmed here.
Information 703-549-1450.

⑬ THE LYCEUM

This Greek Revival style building was built in 1839 to act as Alexandria's cultural center. It served as a hospital during the civil war and a private residence thereafter. Today it houses Alexandria's official museum of history. It contains artifacts from 1749 to the present and features exhibits on architecture, transportation, politics, photography, textiles, and decorative arts. The museum also offers educational programs for various audiences. Information 703-838-4994.

⑭ FRIENDSHIP VETERANS FIRE ENGINE ASSOCIATION

This is one of America's most historic fire houses. There is an extensive collection of fire fighting equipment. George Washington was an honorary captain and purchased the company's first fire engine.

⑮ BLACK HISTORY RESOURCE CENTER

The building was built in 1940 as the first black community public library. With desegregation in the 1960's, the building was converted to use in community service programs. Today the Black History Resource Center is a museum which interprets and documents the history and accomplishments of blacks in Alexandria. Guided tours are scheduled for Tuesdays and Thursdays 10:30am and 11:30am.
The center is open Tuesday-Saturday 10:00am-3:00pm, Sunday 1:00pm-4:00pm.
Information 703-838-4356.

⑯ ALEXANDRIA WATER-FRONT MUSEUM

This museum offers changing exhibits concerning the development of Alexandria's maritime and waterfront activities from 1749 to the present. Information 703-838-4288.

⑰ GEORGE WASHINGTON MASONIC NATIONAL MEMORIAL

Masons throughout our country donated the funds for this memorial to our first president. It was finished in 1932. One of the more interesting exhibits is a replica of the Alexandria- Washington Lodge No. 22, of which George Washington was a member and first Master. Other exhibits include the Washington Family Bible, Washington family murals, and tributes to various chapters of Masons. The memorial is open to the public daily from 9:00am-5:00pm except New Year's, Thanksgiving and Christmas Day. Scheduled tours are offered from 9:15am until 3:45pm.
Information 703-683-2007.

⑱ FORT WARD MUSEUM AND HISTORIC SITE

The fort was the 5th largest fort of 68 built to defend the Nation's Capital during the Civil War. It was armed with 36 guns mounted in 5 bastions. The site now is restored and contains a museum which interprets and preserves Civil War artifacts. The museum also offers educational programs and tours throughout the year. Site

Hours: 9:00am-sunset; Museum hours: Tuesday-Saturday 9:00am-5:00pm; Sunday Noon-5:00pm. Closed Thanksgiving, Christmas, and New Year's Day.

⑲ WASHINGTON'S GRIST MILL

Originally built by George Washington's father, the new mill is a replica of pre-Revolutionary mills. The Mill was on the 2,000 acre tract of land later known as Woodlawn Plantation. It has been said that during one of his inspection trips to the Mill, George Washington caught the cold that brought on his last illness.

⑳ GUNSTON HALL PLANTATION

Built in 1755, the home of George Mason is 20 miles southwest of Washington D.C., on the Potomac River. Mason wrote the "Fairfax Resolves", the first statement defining rights of the colonies. He also wrote the Virginia "Declaration of Rights" which became a model for the Bill of Rights. The interior of the house is one of the most impressive found in any home of the colonial era, including hand carved woodwork designed by William Buckland. From the east door of the house formal gardens may be seen with a central boxwood allee, planted by George Mason. Gunston Hall is open

daily 9:30am-5:00pm except Thanksgiving, Christmas, and New Year's Day. Information 703-550-9220. http://visit.gunstonhall.org/GunstonHall/welcome

㉑ WOODLAWN PLANTATION AND FRANK LLOYD WRIGHT'S POPE-LEIGHEY HOUSE

The land of the plantation was originally part of Mount Vernon and was bequeathed to Eleanor "Nelly" Park Custis and Lawrence Lewis. The construction on the Georgian style house began in 1800 and was completed in 1805. The house features Federal period furnishings. The grounds include extensive lawns, boxwood plantings, and a Colonial Revival garden. Also on the grounds is the Pope-Leighey House. This house, designed by Frank Lloyd Wright, and built in 1940, demonstrates Wright's influence on American architecture with features such as organic unity, free and fluid space, and the relation of the building and construction materials to their natural setting. Special events at Woodlawn Plantation include a Needlework Exhibit in March, a Summer music Series, a Fall quilt exhibition, Needlework Seminars, and a Christmas program. The plantation is open daily from 9:30am to 4:30pm except Thanksgiving, Christmas and New Year's Day.

http://www.nthp.org/index.shtml

㉒ MOUNT VERNON

The estate of George and Martha Washington is the Nation's first and oldest ongoing preservation project. Much of the Mansion is restored to original form with original paint pigments and furnishings. The exhibition area of more than 30 acres contains the outbuildings where activities such as bread baking, weaving, laundry washing, paint mixing, and meat curing. The tomb of George Washington is also contained here. There is a museum shop on the grounds in the former slave quarters. Just outside the main gate sits the Mount Vernon Inn which includes a snack bar, gift shop and restaurant. The non-profit organization which maintains Mount Vernon has never accepted Federal or State support. Mount Vernon is open daily March through October 9:00am-5:00pm, November through February 9:00am-4:00pm. Information 202-780-2000. http://www.mountvernon.org

ADDITIONAL POINTS OF INTEREST
Historical/Museums
African-American Civil War Memorial, Antietam National Battlefield Site, Clara Barton House, Dulles International Airport, Fort Washington , Frederick Douglas Home, Manassas Battlefield , NASA Goddard Space Flight Center, National Building Museum, National

AFRICAN-AMERICAN CIVIL WAR MEMORIAL
Located at 10th & U Streets N.W. in the historic Shaw neighborhood, this memorial honors the 185,000 African American soldiers who fought for the Union during the American Civil War.
Information 202-667-2667

ANTIETAM NATIONAL BATTLEFIELD SITE
This park is the site of a battle during the Civil War. There is a visitor center where one can learn of the historic events of the property and see exhibits. Camping is permitted with reservations. The park is open from dawn to dusk while the visitor center is open from 8:30am-5:00pm.
http://www.nps.gov/anti

CLARA BARTON HOUSE
This is where Clara Barton, founder of the American Red Cross, lived the last 15 years of her life. She dedicated her life to easing the pain of wounded soldiers, despite her dislike of war. In 1868 she learned of the Swiss Jean-Henri Dunant's proposal of the International Red Cross. On return to the United States she fought government officials and public apathy to see the American Red Cross established in 1882. The house was

Museum of Health and Medicine , National Naval Medical Center, Samuel A. Mudd House, Sully Plantation

Churches

Franciscan Monastery and Church, Mormon Temple, National Shrine of the Immaculate Conception, Washington National Cathedral

built in 1891 from boards salvaged from shelters at the Johnstown Flood. The house is usually open daily from 10:00am to 5:00pm; however, ongoing restoration causes some areas to be closed. Information 301-492-6245. http://www.nps.gov/clba

DULLES INTERNATIONAL AIRPORT

Dulles International Airport, Chantilly, Va. serves the general Washington, D.C. metropolitan area. Opened on November 19, 1962 it was the first airport specifically designed for commercial jet aircraft. It is one of two airports in the United States to grant landing rights to the Concorde. The airport houses 17 regular carriers and a number of commuter flight companies. These airlines serve 80 domestic and international destinations. There is parking for 13,300 cars. The Dulles Access Road off of the Capital Beltway gives convenient passage to the airport. Information 703-471-4242. http://www.met-washairports.com

FORT WASHINGTON

The first fort, across the Potomac from Mount Vernon, was begun in 1809, to protect the Nation's Capital from attack by sea. The British destroyed it in 1814. It was soon reconstructed as Washington was retaken. It assumed some significance during the Civil War as fears mounted of an attack of Washington by sea. This fear was not realized. After the Civil War the fort was used as headquarters for the Defenses of the Potomac, transferred to the Department of Interior, transferred back to the War Department, transferred to the Veterans Administration, and now transferred to the Interior Department for park purposes. The park is open daily from 7:30am to dark except December 25. There is a museum open from June 1 to Labor Day. Picnic sites are also available. http://www.nps.gov/fowa

FREDERICK DOUGLASS HOME

Frederick Douglass was born a slave in 1818. He fled from slavery as a young man and worked for abolition prior to the Civil War. In the years after the Civil War, he continued to remind politicians of the promises made to black citizens. He advocated women's rights, comparing their lack of political voice to that of the blacks before Emancipation.

In 1877, Douglass purchased Cedar Hill from which he continued his efforts for equality and justice. After his death in 1895, his second wife Helen Pitts Douglass organized the Frederick Douglass Memorial and Historical Association to keep Cedar Hill as a memorial

84

Stadiums/Sports/Theaters
Arena Stage, Jack Kent Cooke Stadium, MCI Center, Nissan Pavilion, Patriot Center, Robert F. Kennedy Stadium, USAir Arena Washington Convention Center, Wolftrap Farm Park

to Douglass and open to the public. Today this work is continued by the National Park Service. Tours of Cedar Hill include exhibits and audiovisual programs that reflect Douglass's life and work. Tour reservations may be made by calling 703-426-5960 or 703-426-5961. http://www.nps.gov/frdo

MANASSAS BATTLE-FIELD
This is the site of the second battle of Manassas during the Civil War. It is also known as "Bull Run". There is a visitor center where one can learn of the historic events of the property. There are horse trails (horses not provided), and picnic tables. The park is open from dawn to dusk while the visitor center is open from 8:30am-5:30pm.
http://www.nps.gov/mana

NASA GODDARD SPACE FLIGHT CENTER
Experience the thrill of spaceflight. This Branch of NASA oversees actual flight operations of various NASA Projects. It is located just off the Capital Beltway in Greenbelt, Maryland. There is a visitor center, tours and presentations. The facility also offers model rocket launches. Hours 9am-4pm daily; closed Thanksgiving, Christmas, and New Year's. Information: 202-637-7000 http://www.gsfc.nasa.gov

NATIONAL BUILDING MUSEUM
This museum in the Pension Building is located at Judiciary Square between 4th and 5th Streets. It features exhibits on building arts including architecture, engineering, urban planning, historic preservation, construction techniques, and building trades. There are both permanent and travelling exhibits. Tours of the exhibits are offered Tuesday-Friday 12:30pm; Saturday 12:30pm and 1:30pm; Sundays and Holidays 12:30pm. Guided walking tours of the neighborhood are offered on selected days each month. The museum is open 10:00am-4:00pm Monday through Saturday; noon-4:00pm Sundays and Holidays. Closed Thanksgiving, Christmas, and New Year's. Information 202-272-2448. http://www.nbm.org

Points of Interest

Parks

C & O Canal, Colvin Run Mill Park, Glen Echo Park, Great Falls Park, Greenbelt Park, Haines Point, Mount Vernon Trail, Oxon Hill Farm , Prince William Forest Park, Rock Creek Park, Theodore Roosevelt Island

NATIONAL MUSEUM OF HEALTH AND MEDICINE

Contained in Walter Reed Army Medical Center is the National Museum of Health and Medicine, formerly The Armed Forces Medical Museum. The Museum was started amidst the fire and tumult of the Civil War. Museum doctors performed the autopsy on President Lincoln, established the carrier of yellow fever as a certain mosquito, developed and tested an anti-typhoid vaccine, and established a world-wide consultation referral system in World War II. Exhibits at the museum include viewing the body, perspectives from the past, exploring inner space, and the culture of medicine. Group tours are offered by appointment, although the exhibits are open to the public. The museum is open 9:30am-4:30pm Weekdays; 11:30am-4:30pm weekends and holidays. Closed Thanksgiving, Dec. 24,25,31; and Jan. 1.
Information 202-576-2348.
http://www.wramc.amedd.army.mil

NATIONAL NAVAL MEDICAL CENTER

Just south of Interstate 495 on Wisconsin Avenue in Bethesda, Maryland, is the National Naval Medical Center. Commissioned in 1942. It is one of the finest institutions of its kind. It functions as a medical, dental, diagnostic, educational, and research center, and is composed of the following commands: Naval Hospital, Naval Medical School, Naval Graduate Dental School, Naval

School of Health Sciences, Naval Medical Research Institute, and others.
http://www.nnmc.med.navy.mil

SAMUEL A. MUDD HOUSE

Located in Charles County, Maryland, this is where John Wilkes Booth received treatment for his fractured leg after the assassination of President Lincoln. The house today consists of the house museum, gift shop, kitchen (restored) and some outbuildings located on 10 acres. It is located in rural Charles County Maryland. The hours are noon-4:00pm. Opens late March and closes in November.
Special tours are available by appointment 301-645-2987.
http://www.govt.co.charles.md.us/tourissm/attractions.htm

SULLY PLANTATION

The plantation was first owned by Richard Bland Lee, Northern Virginia's first Representative to Congress. It is restored to the appearance during the 1795-1842 period with Federal furnishings. The site includes the kitchen-laundry, smokehouse, and stone dairy. Sully Plantation offers educational programs and special events throughout the year. Information 703-437-1794.
http://www.fairfaxcounty.resource-management.com/sullypla.htm

FRANCISCAN MONASTERY AND CHURCH

The purpose of the Monastery is the preservation and maintenance of Holy Shrines, the support of churches, missions and schools in the Holy Land and for the education of missionaries for these places. The central part of the Monastery, the Memorial Church, is Byzantine in design and houses replicas of sacred shrines from the Holy Land. Underneath the church is a reproduction of a small portion of the catacombs under Rome where Christians in earlier times escaped persecution. The 44 acres of gardens and wooded land that are part of the complex provide a tranquil, contemplative setting. http://www.pressroom.com/~francis.can/

MORMON TEMPLE

The temple itself is closed to non-Mormons, but the visitors center and temple grounds are open to the public. The visitors center has exhibits that explain the history and teachings of the Mormon Church. It is located in Kensington, Md., and is the only Mormon Temple east of the Mississippi River.
http://www.lds.org

NATIONAL SHRINE OF THE IMMACULATE CONCEPTION

The National Shrine of the Immaculate Conception is the largest Roman Catholic church in the U.S. and the seventh largest in the world. It overlooks the campus of the Catholic University of America. Construction began in 1920 on this Byzantine Romanesque building and it was dedicated in 1959. It is noted for its statues, stained-glass windows and mosaics. The Crypt Church is reminiscent of the primitive catacombs, and the many chapels are used for more intimate liturgies. The Shrine seats 3,000 people and the organs have a total of 9,138 pipes. There is also a carillon. Masses are held in the Main Church on Saturday 5:15pm; Sunday 9:30am, 10:30am, noon, and 4:30pm; in the Crypt Church, Sunday 7:30am, 1:30pm, Monday-Friday 7:00am, 7:30pm, 8:00am, 8:30am, 12:10pm, 5:15pm. Guided tours are offered Monday - Saturday 9:00am to 11:00am and 1:00-3:00pm every half hour.; Sundays 1:30 to 4:00pm. The Shrine is open to the public 7:00am-6:00pm Nov. - Mar.; 7:00am-7:00pm Apr. - Oct. daily. Information 202-526-8300. http://www.nationalshrine.com

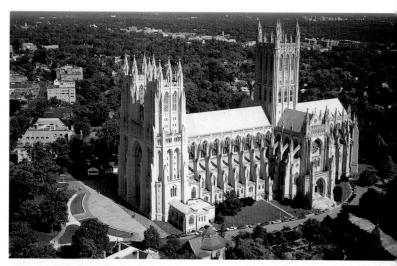

WASHINGTON NATIONAL CATHEDRAL

Officially the Cathedral Church of Sts. Peter and Paul, Washington Cathedral is situated on Mount St. Alban at the intersection of Massachusetts and Wisconsin Aves. Pierre L'Enfant's 1791 Plans for the City of Washington included a proposal for a "great church for national purposes." It has been under construction since 1907 and was completed in 1991. It is the 6th largest cathedral in the world. Under the jurisdiction of the Episcopal Church, it is of Gothic design, the only Gothic cathedral in the nation's capital. Guided tours are available explaining the Gothic architecture. The gardens, especially Bishop's Garden surrounding the cathedral, offer a peaceful atmosphere and setting for this massive edifice. Helen Keller and Anne Sullivan are buried here as is Woodrow Wilson. In the Children's Chapel, one of chapels, everything is scaled to a child's dimensions. The Pilgrim Observation Gallery gives a breathtaking, panoramic view of Washington, D.C. A moon rock presented by the Apollo Eleven crew rests in the stained glass "space" window. Worship services are held Mon. Sat. 7:30am, noon, and 4:00pm; Sunday 8:00am; 9:00am 10:00am (except July and August); 11:00am; and 4pm. The Cathedral is open all year from 10:00am-4:30pm with extended hours (till 9:00 M-F during the summer. Tours are Monday through Saturday 10:00am-3:15pm; Sun. 12:30pm to 2:45pm. Brochures are available in five languages. Information 202-537-6200. http://www.cathedral.org/cathedral

ARENA STAGE

This theater was founded in 1950 by Zelda Fichandler, Thomas C. Fichandler, and Edward Mangum. It is a three-theater complex having an 800 seat, 500 seat and the Old Vat Theater, seating 180. It hosts up to 24 performances per week during a September to June season. It is located at 1101 6th Street S.W., Washington D.C. 20024. Sales 202-488-3300; Protix 703-218-6500
http://www.arena-stage.org

JACK KENT COOKE STADIUM

The Jack Kent Cooke Stadium has been the home stadium of the Washington Redskins since the 1997 Season. It seats 80,114. It is located in Raljon, Maryland.
http://www.princegeorges.com/stadium.htm

MCI CENTER

The MCI Center is a sports complex which opened in 1997. It is the home of Washington Wizards as well as College teams. It has a variety of shops including the Velocity Grill, the Discovery Channel Store and Model Sporting Goods. Information 202-661-5050
http://www.mcicenter.com

NISSAN PAVILION

The Nissan Pavilion at Stone Ridge is a 100 acre site, an amusement park for music lovers. The amphitheater seats 25,000. It hosts everything from an intimate ballet or symphony to a major awards show or concert complete with television or satellite feed. Located at Route 234 and 29 interchanges.
Information 703-754-6400

PATRIOT CENTER

This Theater/Sports Complex hosts a variety of events, from college basketball games to popular concerts. The Patriot center is located on the campus of George Mason University, west of Washington D.C.
Information 703-323-2672.
http://www.gmu.edu/gmu/patriot_center

ROBERT F. KENNEDY MEMORIAL STADIUM

The Robert F. Kennedy Memorial Stadium accommodates professional activities, including sporting events and concerts. It has a seating capacity of 55,000. At the left rear of the Stadium is the Starplex Armory. It is the scene of many successful conventions, trade shows and expositions. The Presidential Inaugural Gala and Ball are held here.

USAIR ARENA

This sports arena is home to the Washington Wizards. It is located at 1 Harry S. Truman Drive, Landover

Maryland, Just off the Capital Beltway.
Information 301-350-3400.

THE WASHINGTON CONVENTION CENTER

This huge center opened in 1982. It has 378,000 square feet of exhibition space, 4 halls, and 40 meeting rooms. It is located at 900 9th street N.W. 20001. It hosts a variety of shows and conventions, often several different programs simultaneously. Only some events are open to the public so call for information 202-371-4200.
http://www.dccovention.com

WOLFTRAP FARM PARK

This national park in Northern Virginia is dedicated to offering concerts of a wide variety of musical tastes. The two theaters, the Barns and the Filene Center host opera, folk music, rock and roll, jazz and blues music. On occasion non musical acts such as comedians and performances such as ballet are offered.
There is a large area for picnics Special accommodations for handicapped can be made b calling 703-255-1800.
To charge tickets on a cred card 703-432-0200.
Information 703-255-1900.
http://www.wolf-trap.org

C & O CANAL

The Chesapeake an Ohio Canal parallels the Potomac River from Cumberland, Maryland, t Georgetown in Washington D.C Its 74 lift locks raise it 605 fee over the course of 184.5 miles

There is a museum a Great Falls Tavern which includes exhibits on the canal's operation. Hiking and bicycling are permitted on the canal's towpath. Camping is permitted in certain areas. Canoeing in the Potomac is discouraged bu allowed. Horseback riding is

llowed from Sains Lock to Cumberland. Information 202-739-4200. http://www.nps.gov/choh

COLVIN RUN MILL PARK

This park includes a millers house, general store, and a dairy barn. It is located at 10017 Colvin Run Road, Great Falls, VA 22066. The park is open daily March through December except Tuesdays. Information 703-759-2771 http://www.fairfaxcountyeda.org /freda/attractions/covin_run.html

GLEN ECHO PARK

This park began as a National Chautauqua Assembly, a meeting place for people to participate in sciences, arts, languages and literature. From 1899 to 1968 the park housed an amusement park. Some of the tracks for trolley cars are still in place. Glen Echo is now a Cultural Arts Park. There are children's puppet shows, picnic areas, and various artwork displays. A major attraction is an original Dentzel Carousel featuring a Wurlitzer Military 165 band organ. It is open for rides on Wednesday afternoons and weekends from May through September. The Spanish Ballroom is used for Contra and Square Dances, Swing Dances, and Ballroom Couple Dances during the summer. Information 301-492-6282. http://www.nps.gov/glcc

GREAT FALLS PARK

On the other side of the Potomac from the C & O Canal at Conn Island and Mather Gorge is Great Falls Park. It contains the Potowmack Canal, started in 1785. This was the nations first canal system, presided over by George Washington. The park is host to a variety of activities including hiking, picnicking, whitewater boating, fishing, rock climbing, and horseback riding.

One can also just go to see the magnificent potomac rush over Great Falls. The park is open from 9:00am to dark every day except December 25. Special tours are conducted from time to time by the Staff. Large groups may schedule tours any time by calling 703-285-2966.

GREENBELT PARK

This park, located just inside the beltway, exit 28 in Maryland, provides a natural setting for hiking, picnicking, and camping.
http://www.nps.gov/gree

HAINES POINT

This park, run by the National Park Service, features an 18 hole golf course, miniature golf, tennis courts, picnic area, and a swimming pool open during the summer. Biking and jogging are also allowed. Fishing is permitted with a valid Washington D.C. license. The park is open from 6:00am-1:00am daily. Information (tennis courts) 202-554-5962, (golf course) 202-863-9007.

MOUNT VERNON TRAIL

You may bike, jog, or walk this 17 mile scenic trail which parallels the Potomac from Washington to Mount Vernon. In addition to the Lincoln Memorial at one end and Mount Vernon at the other, the trail passes the Lyndon Baines Johnson Memorial Grove, The Navy-Marine Memorial, Gravelly Poin Dangerfield Island, Alexandri Jones Point Lighthouse, Bel Haven, Dyke Marsh, Fo Washington, Fort Hunt Par and Riverside Park.

OXON HILL FARM

This working farm off exit 3 of the capitol beltway Maryland, gives the feeling farms in the Maryland an Virginia area at the end of th 19th century. You will see cow chickens, horses and pigs a well as farmhands doing the chores. You may go on a guided tour or wander as you wish

PRINCE WILLIAM FOREST PARK

This park is located 2 miles from Washington along 95 in Virginia. It features pic nicking, bicycling, fishing, hikin and camping. The park als has a Nature Center where par rangers talk about the need fc restoration of the land whic was overfarmed. Informatio 703-221-7181.
http://www.nps.gov/prwi

ROCK CREEK PARK

This park winds its wa throughout Washington an offers a wide variety of activities Picnic grounds, playgrounds tennis courts, hiking trails, an biking trails are provided. Als present are Fort Derussey, For Reno, Fort Bayard (several fort built to protect Washington du ng the Civil War), The Rock reek Nature Center and anetarium (which features nany programs about the natural history and astronomy); Carter Barron Amphitheater (a 000 seat outdoor theater which as a variety of performances uring the summer), Pierce Mill a restored working mill for rinding corn), the Art Barn (an ld carriage house which is sed by a group of artists to display their works), the National Zoo (administered by the Smithsonian Institution), Thompson's Boat House (a place to rent bikes, canoes, and owboats), and Old Stone House. The park is open only in daylight hours. nformation 202-426-6832. http://www.nps.gov/rocr

THEODORE ROOSEVELT ISLAND

The island lies in the Potomac across from the Kennedy Center. It has been through several changes. First called Anacostian from a local ndian name, it has been the property of Lord Baltimore, Captain Randolph Brandt, and George Mason. In 1931 it was purchased by the Theodore Roosevelt Memorial Association o be given as a gift to the American people. A permanent memorial to the 26th President of the United States was begun in 1963. A 17 foot high bronze statue of Roosevelt stands in front of a 30-foot high shaft of granite. Theodore Roosevelt's philosophy of citizenship are inscribed on four 21-foot granite tablets. The island also features hiking trails through three major biological communities.

Swamp, marsh, and upland forest provide a refuge for many native plants and animals including marsh wrens, red-winged blackbirds, kingfishers, and willow, ash, and maple trees.

The parking area is accessible from the northbound lanes of the George Washington Memorial Parkway, on the Virginia side of the Potomac. Telephone 202-426-6922 or 202-285-2598 for information on hours and services available. http://nps.gov/this

INDEX

Index

We the People

insure domestic Tranquility, provide for the common defen
and our Posterity, do ordain and establish this Constitution

Articl

Section. 1. All legislative Powers herein granted shall be
of Representatives.

Section. 2. The House of Representatives shall be compose
in each State shall have the Qualifications requisite for Electors of the m

No Person shall be a Representative who shall not have a
and who shall not, when elected, be an Inhabitant of that State in w

Representatives and direct Taxes shall be apportioned among
Numbers, which shall be determined by adding to the whole Number
not taxed, three fifths of all other Persons. The actual Enumeration
and within every subsequent Term of ten Years, in such Manner a
thirty Thousand, but each State shall have at Least one Represent
entitled to chuse three; Massachusetts eight; Rhode Island and
eight; Delaware one, Maryland six, Virginia ten; North Carol

When vacancies happen in the Representation from any

The House of Representatives shall chuse their Speaker an

Section. 3. The Senate of the United States shall be composed of
Senator shall have one Vote.

Immediately after they shall be assembled in Consequence
of the Senators of the first Class shall be vacated at the Expiration
Class at the Expiration of the sixth Year, so that one third may be chu
Recess of the Legislature of any State, the Executive thereof may make
such Vacancies.

No Person shall be a Senator who shall not have attained
not, when elected, be an Inhabitant of that State for which he shall

The Vice President of the United States shall be President of th

The Senate shall chuse their other Officers, and also a Preside
President of the United States.

The Senate shall have the sole Power to try all Impeachme
of the United States, the Chief Justice shall preside: And no Person

Judgment in Cases of Impeachment shall not extend furth
Trust or Profit under the United States: but the Party convicted sha
according to Law.

Section. 4. The Times, Places and Manner of holding Electi
thereof, but the Congress may at any time by Law make or alter su

The Congress shall assemble at least once in every Year,